The Money Fight

Take Down Your Money Problems,

Slam Your Self Doubt,

and Fight Your Way to

Financial Freedom.

By Paul Halme

The Money Fight

Take Down Your Money Problems, Slam Your Self Doubt, and Fight Your Way to Financial Freedom.

All Rights Reserved

ISBN

Cover design by Sooraj Mathew

Edited by Hilary Jastram & Ashly Wallace

 BOOKMARK

The Money Fight

Resources

Make sure to download all of your free bonuses for buying this book: www.paulhalme.com/mfb

Follow me on Facebook:
https://www.facebook.com/paul.halme

Follow me on Instagram:
https://www.instagram.com/paul.halme/

To hire me to speak, please fill out a form:
www.paulhalme.com/

Make sure to check out my free blogs:
www.paulhalme.com/blog

To my children Chase and Paige. Thank you for inspiring me to do more. My dream is for you to do better than me in all areas of life. But it won't be easy...lol.

Please go through this book and master all the areas, especially the parts about living the life you want. Then pass it down to your kids.

I won't always be here, but what I am teaching you will set you up to live your best life, and that's all a father can do. I love you both, and I am so proud of you.

Contents

Foreword

I'm writing this 30,000 feet in the air, flying across Asia in business class. My feet are up, champagne glass in hand, enjoying my fifty-fourth flight of the year. And the truth hit me like a roundhouse to the head.

I may be good at making money, but I'm much better at spending it. I'm like all of *The Real Housewives of Atlanta* rolled into one. If I stopped working right now, I wouldn't have enough money to retire for very long, and I'm considered by most definitions, to be in the top 1% of 1% of income earners on the planet.

If I can't stop working without the fear of running out of money, I really feel for the average American who works like a dog, day in and day out, with virtually nothing to show for it and little chance to get ahead in life.

I'm what you call a "money dummy." I simply work hard, make as much as I can, and try not to spend it all before my bank account goes to zero.

Genius, I know!

The author of this book is different. When I first met Paul years ago at a business seminar, I was initially intimidated. He had a good six inches on me, and his ears were cauliflowered. (Six inches of height, not length, you sicko). He looked like he could rip my heart out with his bare hands just for looking at him funny.

Thank God he's a nice guy.

It was cool to find out that not only was he a prize-winning fighter, but a former stockbroker turned entrepreneur too. When I met him, he was running a local gym, an online consulting business, and even sold a company years before that!

Over the years, as we've become closer, I've personally witnessed his ability to manage and grow his wealth. He's always teaching me hacks, tips, and cool strategies to get more out of my money. He lives a life of freedom, travel, friendship, and luxury, from a broke fighter to a rich financial fighter. I am just as excited as you are to read this book.

I make more money in a month than most people have the ability to make in an entire year, but you know what they say happens to most big lottery winners. They are broke a couple of years later.

I don't want to play the financial lottery and gamble with my family's future. I want to win this game. I want to keep and grow my money so I can retire sooner rather than later. I'm making a firm and real commitment right here as I type these words: **I WILL WIN THE MONEY FIGHT!**

And I want to do it fast. I want the insider information, don't give me that slow, boring crap that I can find on YouTube. I want real world tactics straight from the cauliflower dude's mouth.

That's why I surround myself with fighters like Paul, people who are better than me at the money fight. It doesn't matter if you are employed or a business owner, Paul's strategies are the same.

Paul is stepping into the ring to help us be free, rich, and happy so that we can help our families and community. So that we can give back to those who are less fortunate. We need his help because this is the biggest and scariest opponent we are ever likely to face.

Through Paul's guidance, experience, and wisdom, let's beat our money problems into submission once and for all. Let's win The Money Fight.

~Father Freedom, aka Mitch Miller

Introduction

Grab a seat. I have a story to tell you.

We all know the American Dream: get a great job, get married, buy the big house, have 2.1 children, a dog named Spot, retire at seventy-two, and everything will be alright.

Or will it? We are raised to conform at an early age and taught about how evil money is. It's normal to live paycheck to paycheck; that's just how it is. Life isn't easy, and money doesn't grow on trees.

George Carlin perhaps said it best when he referenced how crazy it is to believe in the status quo. *"It's called the American Dream because you have to be asleep to believe it."*

Is the American Dream real anymore? I know it was for my grandparents, but times have changed. To me, it's a trap. Even worse, it can become your nightmare.

Trapped in a system that is designed for you to fail.

Now we have to fight for our dreams. The retirement system is broken. We are expected to work our asses off and then hopefully retire. The odds aren't very good that you will even see retirement before you die.

This is the most important fight of your life. I learned to fight at a very young age. It was Christmas Eve, and I was just a kid. My dad, who was my hero, said, "Let's go get pizza." I was so excited; this was so cool. We never did stuff like this, especially during the holidays.

Little did I know, it was just to soften the blow. I can still feel the chill of the cold December air that night in Detroit. We had just gotten back into the car after picking up the pizza, when Dad said, "I am leaving. I got a girlfriend, so you need to take care of your mom and sister."

WTF?? I am eleven years old. From that second on, I hated that man with every bone in my body. Still to this day, even thinking about him makes me angry. He would come and go until my sister turned eighteen. I'm guessing so he didn't have to pay child support. *What a great guy.* All I heard through my teenage years from my parents was: "Money doesn't grow on trees.", "We can't afford that.", and "Money is evil."

Well damn, Dad, maybe if you didn't bang your coworkers and keep getting fired, we would have some money. My dad made good money when he wasn't between jobs, but we were always broke playing catch up from when he was out of work. It was a vicious cycle that we were stuck in.

My dad would always say, "If you want that, then go get a job. We can't afford that." *Well, fuck you, Dad, I will.* I worked my ass off from the age of fourteen to start building my own life. I was gonna show him. *I will go to college and get a better job than you and have more money.*

And I did it.

Graduated college with honors. Moved to Texas to get as far away from him as possible. Got married. Got the six-figure job as a stockbroker. Bought a big house. Had the two amazing kids and, of course, got the dog.

But I still wasn't happy.

Something was missing, and I couldn't figure it out. I did it right, I played the game and won. Why was I feeling so empty? I knew eventually I could retire and go do fun stuff. And in my mind, I kept thinking *got to keep saving so we can enjoy our eighties*. That thought was depressing.

Is this all I have to look forward to? I couldn't stop thinking about it; there must be more. I just couldn't figure out what was missing.

That thought was the catalyst that made me take the plunge into being an entrepreneur. I thought *now; I will be happy for sure.*

Nope…

I was still chasing the dream instead of enjoying the now, and I kept putting a ton of financial pressure on myself.

It was like I had to hoard every extra dollar if I wanted to have a great retirement and not be broke.

Just when I thought it couldn't get worse, my little sister Jane died of complications from an aneurysm. She was only thirty-four and never got to do anything because money was always tight. Next year we will make the trip; how many times have you said that?

This destroyed me. My little sister was an amazing person who deserved to live a long and happy life. I went down a deep, dark hole of depression for a couple of years. I didn't care about anything anymore. I tried to be a good husband and dad, but that two year stretch is a vodka haze that I hardly remember.

Not sure how I kept it together and ran my business. I guess my subconscious didn't want me to fail because I didn't care anymore. I was dead inside. All I wanted was the hurt to go away.

I was so lucky to have an amazing wife and kids who supported me and pulled me out of this. They reminded me of what life is really about.

All my old dreams were gone. I didn't want things. I wanted experiences. Now I needed to turn this around and get my life on track to do the things I wanted to do with the people I love the most.

I had to find a better way, so I read everything I could get my hands on. I talked to people I knew were successful. I studied them to see how they thought. They had done it, so I wanted to see how they did and not waste my time trying everything else.

One thing really stuck with me: it's all about the journey and not the destination. How could I make more of the now without sacrificing the future? Why can't I live a semi-retired life right now?

These questions really got me to shift my mindset. I can have the experiences that I want now if I do a little planning. So, I designed a money plan that I still use today, and that allows me to be happy and take the pressure off. I accepted that everything will never be perfect, and that's okay. I don't give a shit about what the Joneses have.

The concepts in this book can be used by entrepreneurs or people who work in regular corporate jobs. I wrote it so other people can see that they can enjoy life, too, and not be stuck struggling with money issues.

My goal for you in reading this book is to help you get a grip on your money situation so you can live your life and do fun stuff sooner rather than later. To do that, you have to think about money differently. I will show you how. This book is for you if you are caught in the nine to five, counting the days until your retirement, or worried about the money you are making now when you are barely getting by. Or you are an entrepreneur working seven days a week to make your dreams a reality.

Follow the plan and build the life of YOUR DREAMS, not someone else's. This is your money fight, and no one else's.

We are going to go over how to set up your plan and get your money under control and make it work for you. My plan is so simple and automated that you don't have to think about it, and, as a bonus, I will give you my secret tips on how to travel more so that you can enjoy your life NOW! Let's get going.

Chapter 1: Life Can Be Good

Life is good; life is fine.
Life is tremendous all the time.
~Unknown

I know the introduction to the book was a little dark, but it needed to be said to set the tone for what I am going to teach you.

This won't be another boring book about money; this will be a road map for you to use so that you can build the life of your dreams. Life is great now. I can take care of my business, the finances for my gym, my online company, and my family.

I live the lifestyle that I want to live, and I enjoy the freedom to see and do what I want. I can also travel, which is one of my passions. Putting myself in a good financial situation allows me to do everything that I want to do and then some.

But I didn't write this book to talk about me. I wrote this book to talk about you. More specifically, I wrote this book to help you. If you are one of the millions of people who go to bed at night wondering if they will get their financial shit together and are constantly worrying yourself sick about the future, I want to let you in on a little a secret. Getting your finances in order is not as difficult as you might think. It doesn't even involve that many steps!

By reading this book, I want you to learn that your life can be incredibly fulfilling. You can design your perfect life and live it too! The first step to your dream life is designing it. It might be hard for you to believe such a bold claim that you can design and live your perfect life, so I want to share a few client stories with you.

I am so proud of the turnaround that I watched happen and that I helped to facilitate in each of these people's lives. My clients have gotten to a level of success that they didn't know they could reach, and when they did, they weren't even stressed out about money, because they had built a level of comfort with money that they didn't have before.

If you have always felt stress when you think about money, when you are able to replace worry with comfort, it is an astounding emotion that sweeps right through you. No more stress when the first of the month rolls around, and you need to figure out which bills you can pay. No more stress when you get a random car repair bill. No more stress and fighting with your spouse about money.

You will shred your stress because you will be in the right financial place when it comes time to make tough decisions about money, and budgeting will be so much easier.

Check out a few of my client's stories.

Client #1

It was October, a few years ago, when I met one of my clients at an industry event.

I went over how to set up their financial life so that all their hard work would start paying off, and they would begin to reap the benefits.

After the event, this client went home and put into place what I advised him to do, which also happens to be what you will be learning in this book. I would hear from him periodically, so I knew that he was doing the work. The following May, he sent me a message that said: "I really want to thank you. I got a $3,000 bill from the IRS, and I didn't know what to do."

At first, he reverted to the way he traditionally handled unexpected (and sometimes unpleasant) surprises. He completely freaked out.

His normal course of action would have been to panic over this bill because he wouldn't have had the money to pay it. Then he remembered that I had asked him to set up a special account. Luckily, for him, he had done exactly what I had told him to do, and there was a nice surprise waiting for him as a result.

When he looked at that account, the money to pay the IRS was there, and he even had a bit leftover! It was a financial miracle! (No, it wasn't, it was proper planning.) I guarantee that when you follow the system, the same system that I taught him, you will also be able to accumulate money to help get you through the stressful times. Those times that NOBODY wants to deal with.

Close your eyes, and let's imagine you get a $3,000 bill from the IRS, and you don't know what to do because you don't have even close to the amount of money needed to settle the bill. Awful, right? Now, imagine that you must tell your wife about that bill. More than likely, she will get mad at you and blame you for not having a handle on what was supposed to be your responsibility. (This is assuming that you two have an arrangement where you do the bills, and she does the caretaking.) Remember, this is a scenario, and the reverse arrangement with any couple could be true as well.

Whatever the dynamic in your partnership, when you get a notice like that, it causes a lot of fear and anger to float to the surface. Client #1 is proof that you can intercept life's little obstacles and keep going financially without missing a beat. And yes, I realize that after your account takes a ding to the tune of $3,000 that you will need time to recover the money, but Client #1's example shows that a bill like this doesn't have to ruin you.

It might not be an IRS bill that bankrupts you; it might be your vehicle's transmission failing; it could be a bunch of unforeseen medical bills or even a missed payment that wasn't caught for months and is suddenly due. Unfortunately, I can think of many ways that life will cold cock you.

Read on.

Client #2

This dude was making a solid six figures a year when I asked him how much money he had built up in savings.

His response floored me; he said, "Zero." I kept my poker face, but inside I thought, *Damn! I keep hearing about six figure earners not accumulating any money. This is a real problem!* So, I went through how every step of my financial system works. I broke it down in detail for him.

Then I taught him how to do everything. As he left my office, I was hoping that I had reached him, that I had equipped him well enough to make a change.

A month later, I got a message from him.

He was super excited, saying, "Oh my God! I have $1,000 in savings! This is awesome! I didn't have to do anything, but just follow the plan! I've never had that much money in savings in my life!"

This is why my life is great: because I get to help people break their bad money habits and then teach them that they can live the way that they want: i.e., stress free, and without the feeling that a budget is imprisoning them.

I hear stories like Client #2's all too often. People will spend every dollar that they make if they don't move it in to a certain place if they don't assign it a specific job and a new home.

For Client #2, following the system was a baby step, but I guarantee that a couple of years down the road, he is going to have a nice chunk of money put away (if he keeps following the plan). He can use these savings to relieve the stress in his day to day business without worrying about how his bills will be covered.

Client #3

This client represents a huge portion of the clientele that I see, who all make the same mistake. Every single one of them.

Client #3 came to me in a funk about the peaks and pitfalls of entrepreneurship. He shared with me an issue that so many entrepreneurs have to deal with. For one month, he would launch a new product or service, make a bunch of money by selling a ton of packages, but in the next month, or the month after, the money would dry up!

Like so many others that I have helped, this client was living "launch to launch." The problem with this style of business is that between launches, the same financial issues come to the surface, but they are ignored in preparation for the next launch! My client blurted out to me: "Oh my God, I have to get this launch done, or I can't pay my bills!" The stress was oozing out of him over the phone!

When I hear clients share this type of pain, it blows me away because many of these people make so much money. I've talked to high six figure, low seven figure earners, and they're stressed out all of the time. Imagine making seven figures and being stressed to the max about money!?

When I make a plan for "Launch to Launch" clients, my goal for them is to change the way that they think about money. Living between such extreme opposites financially wreaks havoc on you.

You need to break the cycle.

It's entirely possible to use a special system to accommodate the feasts and famines in business, and it is so simple and pain free. I asked Client #3, "Can you take 10% of every dollar that comes into your business when you do these launches and put it away?" He answered me: "Yeah, it's no problem. 10% is easy."

It almost doesn't even make sense to me how much money can pass through someone's hands, and they are not building up their savings.

Stashing just 10% of your income away into an account builds up your savings super-fast. When you do this, you naturally decrease the stress between the launch cycles.

As an entrepreneur, it's super stressful trying to survive from launch to launch. When you use a buffer system, it will remove the insane amount of stress between these feasts and turn the famines into a piece of cake.

In the coming chapters, we are going to talk about where to put your money and how to manage it. You don't need a gajillion dollars to use this process; you can be exactly where you are in your earning potential. You just need to be able to follow directions and stick to the plan.

The guidance I am offering you throughout these pages is all predicated on the income that you are already making. There's no crazy push to hit landslide sales or do anything drastic. Just keep doing what you are doing and implement a handful of steps.

It really is that easy.

Everybody's version of success is different. I designed this program to fit these differing visions. What I advise you to do will work no matter your business model, sales, or income cycle.

After you have been following the steps to build up your accounts, you can customize your success, then go out and get it. Along the way, my team and I will do everything in our power to help you.

No more getting to the end of the month and wondering, *hey, where's all my money*? Or going to the mailbox, retrieving a bill from your doctor, sighing as you resign yourself to handing over everything in your checking account. No more playing the game of saving a little, transfer savings to checking, save a little again and repeat.

When you use this system, gone are the days of being caught unaware and unable to handle events gone awry. If this sounds like a lifestyle that you want, I invite you to keep reading, and I want you to know, your days of being in financial pain are almost over.

Do you ever say one or more of the following things?

- "I don't understand why I don't have any money left."
- "I suck at cash flow."
- "I thought I had more money in my account than that!"
- "Where did all my money go?"
- "How am I supposed to pay bills now?"
- "Will I ever catch up?"

- "Every time I build up little savings, something happens."

If so, then it's time to learn a different way of handling your money.

When you implement my plan, even when the economy goes to crap, you will survive. And yes, we are due for another recession. It's just a matter of time because the market can't sustain a constant "up" environment. It will self-correct, and when it does, the pendulum will swing too far in the other direction. Believe me, though, even that overcorrection won't matter and won't cause you pain because you will have planned for it. I got you. You will weather the storm.

Even better, when you assign destinations for your dollars, you won't be worried about simply surviving the economy's downturns. You will enjoy what you have stashed away, and on the days that financially drop other people to their knees, you will be standing strong.

Extra bonus, while everyone else is running around like headless chickens, you can swoop in and buy up shares and stocks dirt cheap! You can buy a bunch of assets. You can buy properties. You can sink your money into investments and watch them GROW.

You always want to be able to invest money when the market corrects. The worst thing that you can do is buy high and sell low. Later, we will discuss the importance of consistently adding to your investments with dollar cost averaging. This is a game changer and will help you sleep at night when the market sells off. (Don't have any idea what that means? Don't worry. We will go over all of it in the coming chapters.)

We will look at buying opportunities that will build your wealth for the future. During economic downturns, the average person will panic and sell everything. They will be afraid of losing all of their money since they more than likely have no emergency fund set up. But that will not be you. You will be in a position to make money moves.

Chapter 2: Your First Steps

"Money doesn't buy happiness.
Some people say it's a heck of a down payment, though."
~Denzel Washington

I want to make sure that what I am about to tell you is as simple as possible because the more complicated the process is, the harder it will be for you to stick to the plan.

Now, don't freak out, but it's time to talk about the dreaded "B" word.

Yep…. Budgets!

Budgets suck, and they are certainly no fun. So, let's look at them in a different way. I like to make a game out of managing my money, so it doesn't feel like grueling, punishing work.

Step 1) Open a business savings account (if you are not a business owner, then make sure to open a personal savings account today. You can even set this book down (as long as you come back to it) and go open one now.

Step 2) Resolve to put a dollar a day in your newly established savings account. Just start small. No, it might not seem like much, but that's the whole point. You have to take action and get started.

Doing this might feel like you're taking a small step, but it will make a huge difference in the long term. Understand this step has to be small so that you will start.

I'm serious when I tell you to make it a game. After you open your savings account, set it up to automatically move one dollar per day into it. I know that you are going to laugh and think that it's a joke to save one measly dollar per day, but if you set up an account and start putting a dollar a day away, then you're going to be that much closer to your goals.

Don't say to yourself: *Once I get "X amount," then I'll start saving*. You need to accept right now that your savings will never be built that way, and it will also never last that way.

How do I know this?

Because EVERYONE says that they are going to put money away and not touch it. EVERYONE. And guess what? Most people never even take that first step to create an account, much less move that single dollar to their savings. Now, back to your super awesome savings plan. Once the savings account is set up, we're going to make it fun.

Ask yourself, *If I put aside 5% of my company's gross sales this month (or 5% of my salary for my non entrepreneur friends), is that going to make or break me?* Assess where your pain level is when you answer this question. If the pain level is too high at 5%, maybe you can say, *I'm going to transfer 1% of my company's gross sales this month into our savings account*.

You can mess around with that percentage and try to manage the pain level at 1% or 2%. The goal is to make sure that you feel a stretch, but you don't feel pain with this small, but possibly significant, percentage of gross revenue. If you reach a point where you feel good, as if you are barely affected at all, it's time to increase your savings percentage.

As I stated before, if you're feeling too much pain, then you can dial down the percentage. I can't stress this enough. Don't force yourself into a situation where you won't be able to sustain your plan. You want to pick a number that is achievable, one which slightly pushes you, and then follow through with hitting that percentage each and every month.

You don't want to create frustration for yourself by really straining to get that money into that savings account. So, starting small is the key.

Frustration leads to discouragement, and discouragement leads to you to the abandonment of your new financial plan. Set yourself up for success, not failure.

Get brutally honest with yourself. It's not he or she who stashes away the most money who wins; it's he or she who can hit their monthly savings goal the most consistently that wins! (With your new automatic transfer, the answer should be that you don't need to worry about it because the saving is done automatically for you.)

The goal that I want to see you attain is to build up a six month buffer. Meaning, if you have $10k/month in expenses, you would save $60k. Yes, I know that sounds like a lot, but you will get there. Stick with me as the numbers start to seem crazy; we are going to improve your money mindset and show you the way to build up these savings accounts.

It's highly improbable that you will be able to put away the entire six month buffer amount that you need in one shot, but the regular automatic transfers should get you there painlessly and as soon as responsibly possible.

Once you've met that six month goal, you can start planning all kinds of new excitement for your life! You can prepare for retirement, improve your business (maybe even scale it!), and take trips, etc.

The truth is that you will be able to do whatever you want because you will have the financial freedom to do it. After you have hit your six month buffer goal, then every quarter take half of whatever you've built up in the account, (**OVER your six month buffer**) and put that toward your retirement account. **Example: To reach $60k in your savings account.** Your gross deposits are $10k. 10% of that is $1,000 per month.

At the end of the three month quarter, you will have $3,000 built up, and at the end of the year, you will have $12,000 dollars in your savings account. Now won't that take the edge off when you get a random bill that used to freak you out?

I know what you're thinking, *it's gonna take me five years to hit my goal.* At this rate, it will, but here is where you will begin to look for ways to scale it up and get to your goal faster. Make it a game.

15% of profits=$4,500 per quarter, so now you would be at $18,000 annually added to your savings. Now we are at just a little over three years to hit the 60k. You tighten up your systems, and now you are at 20% profits = $6,000 per quarter, so no, you would be at $24,000 annually added to your savings. Boom! Only two and a half years to hit that number.

How much will your life change when you have that 60k emergency fund sitting there? Trust me; it will change a LOT.

Now that we have finished the game of funding your emergency account, we will move onto growing your retirement account so that you're not a broke old person struggling to pay the bills in your golden years. We will go a lot deeper into this later in the book, but here is the plan's basic framework.

Using the gamified example above, the $6,000 that is going into your savings account every quarter will now be split into two ($3,000 and $3,000 respectively). Simply take half of that $6,000 (or $3,000 if you're keeping score) and move it to your brokerage account and use it to fund your retirement account. So, after the first savings distribution, after you have 60K in your savings account, you will now have $63,000 in your business savings and $3,000 in your brokerage account. Your savings account will keep growing since you are adding half of the quarterly amount.

At the end of the year, you now have $72,000 in your savings account (60K plus the 3k per quarter) and $12,000 in your brokerage account. I want you to go back and read that again. Let it sink in. You are taking control of your financial future. In three and a half years, you have built an $84,000 foundation. This number can be a lot higher, depending on how much you make. A $30,000 gross with 20% profits would put you at about $120,000 in savings and 60K in your brokerage and retirement accounts in roughly less than three years. Now, do you see why I love money math so much!?

And why I turn saving into a game!? These numbers are real, and I can guide you to them. We are going to go deeper into how the whole system works. Once you see it all spelled out, it's pretty easy to see where your money is going to be. That's your long term retirement money. You can't touch it. It's gone. Consider it as though it's not even there. It has moved from your savings to your long term investing account. The other half of the savings surplus money can be allocated to other areas. Does your business need improvements? Do you need to fix walls, paint the place, or get new equipment?

In the example above, you would have $1,500 in the account just from the most recent quarter. See how fun this is? Money just starts to appear. Maybe you don't need any of those things if everything's going really well. So, then you can reward yourself and do something fun. One of the most important reasons why I am teaching you these financial shortcuts is so that you are not stuck when you're older. Don't look forward to enjoying life when you're seventy years old. Enjoy life now while you're planning and building for the future.

You never know what could happen and when your time might be up. It could all disappear in a snap of the fingers, and the worst part of it is that you never did anything fun.

My little sister passed away at thirty four years of age due to complications from an aneurysm. She always planned on doing stuff later. Well, for her, later never came. Losing her had a huge impact on me. I decided from that day onwards; I would do what I wanted to do now, not later.

One final note I would like to leave you within this chapter is that once you have deposited/transferred your money into your savings, pretend that it's not there, aka never mess with it. It doesn't exist.

The ONLY exception when you might use it is in the case of a true emergency is like taxes, a medical situation, or dire circumstances equating to life or death. If you go through something like that, then you absolutely can go into that six month buffer and take the money out. In the absence of a true emergency, the goal is to pretend that that money doesn't exist. That money is not to be used for a small purchase that you could cover with your regular operating expenses.

I know that this is going to take some getting used to, but practice will make perfect, and it will also build up the money in your account faster than you think!

To keep you motivated, please see my special gift to you below, an online Investment Calculator that calculates your potential monthly savings goal. For example, if you are making $50,000, it will tell you how much 1% or 2% savings would be. You get the picture.

When you use this Investment Calculator, you can assess the magnitude of your decisions and how they are affecting your business. You will be able to see how changing your *savings percentage from 1% to 3% will affect the big picture.* If you are generating $25,000 a month gross, for example, those percentages will come to life when you use this Investment Calculator. It will show you what you are doing with your funds and what your next step for stashing cash will be.

This Investment Calculator is going to motivate the hell out of you and get you super excited. So, make sure to click the link below and start playing around with it.

www.paulhalme.com/investment-calculator

Chapter 3: Ass Kicking & Perseverance

"There are two ways to do anything,
the right way, and again."
~Navy Seals

When you try to save money using dollar amounts, it gets super daunting, stressful, and most of the time, you just don't do it.

That's why I advise people who are looking to properly manage their money to always try to hit goals in percentages. Percentages are easier to think about, easier to move, and easier to simply digest. It takes the emotions out of seeing dollar signs.

Let me explain.

If I told you that you had to move $1,000 a month right now to a savings account, you'd likely question me, thinking, *Oh, I don't know if I could do that*. But if I said, *you need to move 10% of every sale into your savings account*? That's a far easier directive to wrap your mind around.

It's easier to make a commitment to working with a percentage. In contrast, working with dollars scares the shit out of most people (except people who have grown up with a good education in wealth.) People who have been educated properly on wealth and money management are the exception to the rule because most people have been raised with the motto, "Money doesn't grow on trees," as I started way back in the introduction of this book.

Back to percentages: you're not going to go broke because you're only taking a *percentage* of your sales and moving it over. Like I said in Chapter 1, the savings percentage that you stash away should feel uncomfortable, but not painful.

Start with as small a percentage as you want. There's no shame in doing 1%. Yes, 10% is a good starting point, but the goal is to begin with a sustainable starting point, so the habit of saving is established.

I've told people, "A dollar is easy. If that's all, you can do today, perfect. Do 1% when you are ready, then 2%, 3%, and so on." Begin where you can, with the goal to build.

As you build up that percentage, you're going to see your life change. When that number gets above 10%, I promise you; you'll be able to deal with stress in a whole new way. You'll be able to deal with unexpected bills, surprise invoices, and "out of nowhere" expenses.

Remember, getting over the 10% mark will change your life. You will start building up real money in your accounts. Here's another bit of reassurance. If you have bumped your savings percentage up to a certain level, it doesn't mean you that you need to keep it there.

As I said, you can always adjust it; the percentage that you are committing to is flexible. You can move the percentage up and down so you can live with your choice, while still being somewhat aggressive.

When I share with clients that if something crazy were to happen, they always have the option to change that percentage, it makes them feel better. The percentage is not set in stone. So, if you're at 10% and your business has a couple of hard months, then, yes, you can move the number down from 10% to 9%, 8%, 7%, 6%, or even 5%. Whatever you can live with.

As you move your percentage around to whatever it needs to be, you still need to keep something going all the time. You are making a commitment to long term planning for you and your family's financial future.

Pay Yourself First

You deserve to get paid first.

I know not many business owners think this way, and that it is a mindset shift, but it is a critical one. You need to adopt this mindset so that you can stick to your new financial plan more easily. You are going to start to build momentum by beginning to put money away, and you are going to build good habits to have a stronger financial future. The biggest focus needs to be on yourself to reach your financial goals.

I like to compare the process of shifting your mindset to the process of building up your endurance for running. (Side note: Nobody likes running. If they tell you they do, they are lying to your face, or they are just crazy…). Let's say that you've been running regularly for a long while; you've endured months and months of regular running. At this point, a long run of ten miles isn't impossible for you because you've conditioned yourself by building up your tolerance for exercise. I repeat you are CONDITIONED. This is code for: your body is not going to be in pain the next day.

Now, let's say you have been following your routine of running; you're doing it all the time, but then all of a sudden, you stop for three or four months. You are injured, or a family emergency happens, or whatever, your routine is gone. What do you think is going to happen if you try to start back up again after months of being away?

It hurts like hell when you get back out there and start pounding the pavement again. Right!? You're sore. It's hard to walk. Every step causes deep aches in your muscles, shins, and feet. In short, it's horrible. And don't forget, you have to start at square one again so you can build back up to the endurance level you were at before. What can we learn from this analogy?

First, if you start running, you can never ever stop (that's why I do Jiu-Jitsu). More importantly, it shows us that we can't just abandon our regular conditioning and then pick up where we left off and expect to be in the same state. The same principle applies to money. You've got to keep the momentum going. If you have to change the percentage, that's fine. If you've got to make some tweaks, whatever; you can recover.

Just. Don't. Stop.

Every month, without fail, you need to be saving money for your future. So, stop thinking small because there's an infinite supply of money out there, and you can tap into it as you continue to grow and reach new levels. There is always more.

As you level up your business, you will meet more people than you ever imagined, and this phenomenon will keep repeating.

You will level up again, and you will meet more people again, which will translate into earning more and more money.

How? The larger your network, and the more people you meet, the more business you can do. This is one of the coolest parts of doing business: just when you have grown accustomed to your new level of growth. IT WILL HAPPEN AGAIN! Growth is viral!

Believing in this process is called an abundance mindset. The abundance mindset can be applied to every part of our lives; all you need to do is believe that there is always more than enough out there.

More than enough prospects, more than enough money, more than enough time, more than enough love. When you adopt an abundance mindset, it means that you will always have more than enough in whatever area of life you are talking about.

Remember this: We set the limits on what we can attain. Let's say that again…**WE SET THE LIMITS ON WHAT WE CAN ATTAIN.**

Some people may earn way less than you, and some people may earn 500 times more than you. The only difference between individuals is that some of them use an abundance mindset and put it to work!

They believe that the money is out there and that they are entitled to more than enough of it for the amount that will allow them to take care of all their needs, and their family's needs. Guess what? That same money is yours for the taking, too. You just need to BELIEVE in this idea, too.

Better your business; better your mindset; better yourself, and when you do this, you will make more money. It doesn't make sense to live life safely, so ask for that raise. Get that bonus. Sign up more clients. Run your business so that it's more profitable. There's always more money out there, no matter what you have to do to get it.

Maybe you need to tweak your systems and processes. Maybe you need to create an opportunity for passive income. Whatever you need to do, drop the scarcity mindset. Stop thinking that "Money doesn't grow on trees" or that other people earning money means that there is less money for you to earn.

It's not easy as pie. Quite frankly, metaphorically speaking, money DOES grow on trees. You just need to find the right trees. They are out there! And you can find them because you deserve it. Never forget that you deserve to have everything that you want in this life.

What we have talked about in this chapter just skims the surface of the mindset shift that you will need to adapt to experience the success that you want and deserve. An abundance mindset will change your life. The sooner you apply it, the sooner you can benefit from it, so start today.

Here's a tool that can help you to acquire an even deeper foothold of this very prosperous mindset. Download this mindset and abundance training video to jumpstart your luck and your life. In it, you will learn about the mindset changes you have to make to get to the next level.

And here's a huge takeaway for you: if your mind is fucked, then you're going to have a hard time even starting. So, to get to where you want to be, whether it's in your business, your relationships, or your health, you need to work on yourself first.

I want you to have this training as my gift to you for buying my book, but more importantly, I want you to have it because I know it will change your life. Before we can make any real headway, we have to deprogram all the crap we were fed as kids about money.

Remember, nothing is more critical than this mindset: you deserve it. You deserve to pay yourself first and design a successful life for you and your family with the least amount of money stress possible.

Start telling yourself that every day. Repeat this to yourself over and over again: *I deserve it!* Then go to this link, check out the mindset training, and then move on to the next chapter.

www.paulhalme.com/mfb

Chapter 4: Get The Money That's Out There Without Draining Your Bank Account

"If you don't get serious about your money,
you will never have serious money."
~Grant Cardone

Before we immerse ourselves in the topic of this chapter, I need to revisit what we just talked about in the last chapter.

You have to understand that you deserve the money that you are working so hard for. Even beyond understanding, you have to accept this as fact. Being deserving of money needs to be your mindset. You can't afford to think small like *"Rich people suck."* Or *"I'll be fine just getting by."* I can promise you that you will not get anywhere close to where you dream of being with those limited, scarcity driven mentalities. You deserve this success and all the money that will come with it.

So, do the mental mindset work to get yourself where you need to be, in terms of your abundance mindset. Please don't tune this out. We are programmed to think in a scarcity mindset from the very beginning of our lives. The people around you don't want you to do better than them, so they will keep planting these seeds of doubt in your mind.

As you start to build up your finances, you will notice the people closest to you will say, *"You've changed."* Well, just smile and say, *Yes, I have*! You need to change to become the person who believes that they deserve more money. Not the person who complains that money doesn't grow on trees, and rich people are evil.

Those are self-limiting beliefs; they are like a virus. They will keep growing and growing if you don't eliminate them as soon as possible. I try to lift my friends up, but I can't make them believe in themselves. They need to believe in themselves for any growth to happen.

You have to keep training your mind to push through these mental barriers. Dr. Shannon Irvine does an amazing job of this on her podcast. She is always breaking down how our subconscious is secretly guiding all of our decisions. This was a major breakthrough for me. If you always think you're broke or you always complain about bills, then your subconscious will keep reminding you. When you change this mindset and start to focus on abundance and growth, then you start to see a huge shift.

Talk about money. Think about money. It's not evil. Think of all the good things you could do in the World if you had more money? Who could you help? What legacy could you leave for your family? Now close your eyes and imagine logging into your investment accounts, and seeing your total dream balance, let's manifest the shit of out this.

What is the amount you dream about building up to? Write it down on the line.

Think big: $_____.

Even when I was a stockbroker crushing six figures a year, in my head, I was always broke. I couldn't escape it. I never had any money left at the end of the month. Every time I got a raise, I found a way to spend it. The only good thing was I had my 401k auto investment set up, so I never saw the money move. You will see how this is a key piece of my system later on in this book.

After I made the jump to full time entrepreneur, I still had the same mindset and no extra money at the end of the month. I was subconsciously sabotaging myself.

When I broke through this mental barrier, my company made the jump to over seven figures a year. A number that I had long told myself was impossible. Why was it impossible? Because I was getting in my own way and self-sabotaging my success. Here is a link to a free course that Dr. Irvine offers on brain priming: https://drshannonirvine.com/mindyourbusiness

Legacy Mindset: The Building Block

You want to make sure that you have an awesome retirement, right?

Maybe you want to give to charity, and maybe you want to help your children buy their first home? There are so many things you want to do, so I invite you to start to think about what they are. Making the goals for your finances bigger than yourself is the gist of the Legacy Mindset. You've got to think about the long term bigger picture instead of thinking paycheck to paycheck, launch to launch, or even month to month.

If you are always thinking about just making it to next month, you are always going to run out of money. You have to set goals and always be thinking ahead. Big picture thinking involves asking questions like: *What do I need to do to be at a new level in one year?*

When you are considering the action that you need to take, make your goals a game to get to the next level. What will life look like in year three when your accounts are full, and the pressure is gone? When an unexpected bill comes, you just pay it and move on. What amazing trips will you have taken? How about in year five, ten, or twenty? See how fun this can be!?

Instead of always worrying, you are now building a life of abundance and getting the chance to enjoy it. I go on the most epic vacations now, and they are almost all free. We will get into that in the bonus chapter about travel.

This is how you reverse engineer your thinking. Do the money math, and you'll figure it out.

It's Not a Legacy Plan if You Can't Have Fun

While you are planning, you have to do little things for yourself along the way.

You have to take the trips, see what you want to see and do what you want to do. Look at it this way; if all you ever do is save a butt load of money and live to retire at seventy years old, what is the point? If you make it to seventy without having spent a dime, and having experienced nothing, here's a hard truth to swallow; when you die, your wife is going to have a wonderful new life with her new spouse, and you're going to be the one funding it.

Or vice versa!

Here's another scenario: what if you get to the age of 70 and then are too sick or disabled to go anywhere or do anything...or what if a week after you retire, you die? Please refer to scenario number one, where your wife and her new husband are having a blast with your money.

Let's take a moment and think about that...yup, it is actually as terrible as it sounds. Don't be that person. When I think about my money goals this way, it makes me pledge to enjoy my life. I'm going to do what I want to do while I'm building for my future. I'm not waiting until I'm 70 years old to take the trips that I've always envisioned.

You can break the stigma around savings by managing your money in a way that gives you the freedom to spend it.

Let me assure you; there's nothing wrong with enjoying your money and even spending some of it as long as you can still meet your financial targets. Being financially responsible is not about depriving yourself. If spending your money on an item makes you feel good, and you enjoy it, then do it. I mean, as long as it's legal, get out there and do what you want to do. Enjoy it without worry! Guilt free spending is a freedom that not many people enjoy in life, but it IS possible.

Life shouldn't be boring; it should be fulfilling. You should be able to enjoy it now. If you're an entrepreneur, you will definitely understand this next piece of guidance. If you have plenty of money coming in already and don't need to work on improving your marketing and sales, then please skip ahead to the next chapter, and let's start making money moves. If you need to make more money, please make sure to read this chapter.

The Dynamic Duo: Marketing & Sales

Once you firmly believe that you deserve what's coming to you, you will learn the two things that will earn you more money.

Dollars to donuts, the solution to getting more money in your life will be found in these two things. Sales and marketing need to be combined to maximize your efforts in earning money. We need to blend these two critical areas into one powerful tool to send your business efforts into the stratosphere. Let me address a question that you might already have: *Paul, why do marketing and sales matter when you're talking to me about growing my money?*

In my opinion, there is no faster way to get more money than by getting better at marketing and sales, unless of course, you win the lottery. So, don't cut short your effort in these two areas. Marketing is what will bring new customers to your business, and new leads are the lifeblood of business. If you want more money in your life, then you need more leads in your life, which means that you need to get better at marketing.

Of course, you need to make sure that the leads you attract are going to be the kind of quality that will give you your ideal client, but this should only motivate you more! Coupled with marketing is its spouse: Sales. They are like peanut butter & jelly. What good are leads if you can't sell to them?

We all know that in any company, the highest paid people work in sales, but salespeople sometimes get a bad rap as being low down, cutthroat, and so desperate that they will do anything, even unethical things. Sales don't have to be sleazy, though, and in fact, they shouldn't be sleazy! All that consumers are looking for are solutions to their problems, and selling a product is simply providing these people a solution. So, I truly believe that sales should be a sleaze free zone.

Developing these two skillsets (marketing & sales) will allow you to make more money, which will allow you to put more money away without having to live on a budget that is tighter than a mouse's ear. Since you are focusing on putting more money away, it only makes sense that you should implement tactics to increase your earnings (a.k.a. feed the beast).

Not to mention, we all know that living on a budget sucks and pushes us into a scarcity mindset. It is easy to stay stuck in this mindset when you feel like you have less money at your disposal, and you want to take whatever steps possible to ensure that you don't feel this way. What better way is there to overcome a scarcity mindset than establishing processes for bringing more funds into your business?

When you do this, you will feel better about living by the dreaded "B" word, but before I go on, I want to pose a question: why in the world do people get so uptight at the thought of living on a budget? Simply put, when you live on a budget, all you think about are the things that you have to give up and the things that won't fit INTO the budget! You become obsessed with the little things that you can't have anymore.

In my eyes, yes, you should have a baseline budget; you should know what you need to earn each month to cover your bottom line. After this is covered, though, you should strive to always be thinking of ways to make more money—not to buy more things.

How can you build up your financial accounts to the point where you can buy whatever you want and remain stress-free (within reason)? The answer is setting up your plan and following it every day! So, forget budgeting. Budgeting sucks. That's why we're going to switch your thinking to a little something that I like to call the Legacy Mindset.

Instead of focusing on what you can't have, which is what happens when you live on an established budget, I want you to switch your thinking to revolve around how you can make more money for saving for your legacy.

A lot of us choose entrepreneurial life because we want something different. We feel different. We like our autonomy and our liberation from the "nine to five." So, to help with your awesome entrepreneurial life, I want to give you the best marketing and sales tips that I have for making a positive and profitable impact on your business.

Marketing Tips: Getting and Staying Top of Mind

If you're going to get the right message to the right market, you need to know a couple of things first: Who is your market?

This might seem like a daunting question, but there are ways to answer that aren't complicated. Of course, I will give you a gift at the end of this chapter to help you identify what you need to know, but please be aware: the internet contains every answer to every question that you have. You can look up different avatars and even define your avatar. What's an avatar? An avatar is your perfect customer.

After figuring out your avatar, what is the message that this perfect customer needs to hear? What questions are they asking, and what problems are they experiencing?

Once you have those two key pieces of knowledge dialed in, you need to obtain and leverage free and paid traffic. This means Facebook, Instagram, YouTube, Twitter, and any other platform where your customers will be. This next part is pretty simple, but it will require some refinement. Your social media posts and the content will need to contain the message that your avatar wants to hear (i.e., the solution to their problems).

Resist the urge to throw a bunch of money at your ads early on. Start with a bunch of organic content, garner some results, and keep track of what content gets the most engagement. If you are in tune with the right market, then you will see positive results that you can build on. You can keep amplifying your results, which will create what I call a compound effect.

The aim of your marketing is to always keep pushing, pushing, pushing, and compounding your results. Post more and post often!

Be Seen Everywhere.

Okay, you are creating and posting free organic content, but what KIND of content is really resonating with your ideal audience?

Since you have been tracking the pieces of content that have garnered the most engagement, you will want to use this style of content and then amplify them with paid ads. Facebook and Instagram make this really easy to do. You can literally implement ads for a dollar a day per piece of content. I don't want to get too technical on you, but I do want to give you two simple tips that will make a huge difference in your business.

Make sure that your Facebook pixel is on your website and make a custom audience of people who visit your site.

Make a custom audience of everyone who has engaged with your Facebook business page.

Then take these two custom audiences and create a saved audience to run your ads to. Doing this will get you the most bang for your buck.

If you are confused or feel like this tactic is a little over your head, don't worry, I am not going to leave you hanging. There is a link to a video I made just for you on how to do this at the end of this chapter.

Sales Tips: Ask The Right Questions And Dig Deeper

The first and best question you can ask your prospect is, "What made you decide to reach out today?"

Something pushed them to reach out to you, find out what it was. This question is very impactful because when the prospect replies, they are telling you their motivations in their own words. This is important because you are not telling them why they have sought you out and why they are now standing in front of you; they are telling you. One of the most critical actions we can take as salespeople is to listen.

The next question will let you go even deeper and make it significantly easier to close sales. "Why is that important to you?" There is always a deeper reason why they reached out, and they will not say it right away. By digging deeper with this question, you will find out what they are really trying to fix. This will make a huge difference in your sales. Just sit back and listen to what they are saying.

One person might be on blood pressure medication, and another person might want to hold onto their house. Either way, they want help moving towards their goals.

Let's say you own a gym, and somebody walks in, and after a bit of small talk, you ask, "So, what made you reach out today?" You might hear back: "Oh, I've been thinking about getting back in shape." At first glance, it might seem like you've got your answer, but you have only scratched the surface. You haven't gone deep enough.

So, let's burrow into the second level. That's when you ask this question: "Why is that important to you?" The response you get back will really lead your sales process forward.

Now, your prospect really opens up and says, "You know, I'm on blood pressure medication. My doctor says I gotta lose twenty pounds, or my life expectancy is gonna be a lot shorter. I got grandkids. I want to see my grandkids grow up. I don't want to die."

That's quite a different experience than what you initially told in their first answer, right? At this point, you have gone so deep with your prospect; you're not even talking sales anymore. Now you're consulting them on their life. You can apply what they have told you to your responses to help them make a good decision, a decision, and one that will change their life and help them reach their goals.

"So, your doctor said you need this. You need that. Well, guess what? I offer this that and the other program. We're going to get you to your goal. We're going to accomplish what you want, and you are going to feel better. Everything that you want you're going to get."

Now, that prospect is listening to you because you have taken them from worrying about dying young to showing them a real solution…right in front of their face.

So, you continue, "It's only going to cost you this much per month, and they're nodding. They're listening to you, so you keep going. "Sound good?"

This is when you wait for them to answer. The process is simple. Once you have the answers to question one and two, it's truly as simple as presenting an offer that matches your prospect's needs and solves their problem.

That's why I love real sales calls and in person interactions, because I can match up the prospect's problems with my solutions, and all I have to do is listen to them! No matter what business you're in, you're trying to help people. You could run a gym; you could be in consulting.

Let's look at another example of really drilling down. If you're a marketing agency talking to a small business owner, they might tell you: "I need more customers and more leads." You're on the right track with that info, yes, but you still need more from them to identify their true pain point and offer reassurance.

"Okay, I hear you, Mr. Prospect. You need more customers and leads. So, tell me what problem do you solve? We can flip the script on the second question we would normally ask and redirect the answers we need toward their clients: "Why is that important to your prospects?" Wait for them to answer, and when they do, then you can say: "Ok great, now that we know the problems that you solve and why that's important to your clients, we can move forward.

"Let's put together a campaign that gets you in front of your perfect avatar and use this messaging. This will get you more leads that will turn into more customers." Do you see how the messaging has to stay consistent with what your customers need? You've got to ask the right questions of your prospect and listen to them. Don't be afraid to go deeper and provide a solution that is best for them.

I've given you quite a few tools to start better understanding your sales and marketing processes. Here's another one. Click on the link that will take you to a sales and marketing funnel cheat sheet PDF that I have found invaluable in my own business. This sheet lists the main traffic sources for marketing, and you can use it to build out your personal traffic plan.

You'll notice I've also included the avatar sheet, which helps you identify your perfect customer, too. Once you download these PDFs, make sure you use them.

Finally, make sure to watch the video on the bonus page to learn how to use the Facebook pixel and making your custom audience to get in front of more of your dream prospects.

Downloading these sheets is yet another step in leveling up your business and getting you closer to claiming the money that's yours. The money you deserve.

www.paulhalme.com/mfb

Chapter 5: Money Moves

"You have to make the right money moves
to get what you want in life."
~Paul Halme

Similar to when we talked about percentages over dollars, this chapter is going to cover money math before money moves...and what the difference is.

Money math and money moves are two of the most important things you will continuously do to make sure you reach your financial goals. Getting these two forces rolling will set you up for long term success.

The primary lesson that I want to teach you in this chapter is that moving large sums of money is scary, but before you can move a penny, you have to establish peace of mind prior to proceeding with your money moves. We talked earlier about how you deserve to get paid first, and now that we have established that mindset, let's get to the fun stuff.

You have to do the MONEY MATH first so that you can ensure that your MONEY MOVES are easy to make. This is how money math works.

You have to work on building up your monthly savings percentages until you can get up to at least 10%. Again, do not feel the pressure to start at 10%; simply start where you can, and then build.

Start at 1% and keep moving that percentage up, make it into a game. Can you get to 3%? Then 5%? And eventually 10%? At each percentage point, you will see more and more money accumulating and compounding. All of this progress is a beautiful thing.

Money Math: The Early Years

I can still remember sitting in my eighth-grade math class with Mr. Hoftiezer.

I was stuck at my desk trying to answer two eternal questions: which train (train A or train B) will get to the station first…and *Why in the fuck do I care about this?* I know I am not the only one who also thought: *How is this gonna make a difference in my life?*

I hated math in school because it didn't make sense to me, but fortunately, I also happened to love money. Math, money. Money, math. It's remarkable how, when you simply apply context to something that you hate, it suddenly becomes something that you love. So, despite the train analogy, I am very thankful for the lessons Mr. Hoftiezer taught me, he was a great teacher.

Math is beautiful when you learn about how money works, how to move it, and how to accumulate it. I'll do that math all day long, but between you and me, I still don't know which train is going to reach that imaginary station first.

I'm all for people enjoying what they are learning about and making it relevant to their lives. So, while we are here spending this time together, I want to address the elephant in the room.

So many people think that what I am talking about saving money doesn't apply to them. They say to me, and maybe you are even thinking this, too: *Paul, I don't make that much money, so I can't do your program.*

Pardon my French, but I call bullshit!

Do you have a dollar in your bank account? Well, you must. After all, you bought this book! Start with a dollar, then as you grow, that dollar can turn into a percentage, and that's how you save. You keep building even off of an amount as small as a dollar. It does make a difference!

The next trick is to then assess how much money you have left at the end of the month and then look for one bill that you could get rid of. It's pretty exciting to even be considering this option! What's one thing you could dump? There is ALWAYS an extra bill that you don't need anymore. When you cut a bill, it allows you to start saving for your future. Next, this new money starts to increase the balance in your profit account, and before long, your long term investment account grows!

There are going to be times when you don't want to put the money away. I understand that you have to pay off some bills. That's okay. Pay off the bills, but still, put something away every month. The saying, "Every little bit helps," was made for this scenario. Here's another philosophy: It doesn't matter how you feel about saving; you just have to do it. It's that important.

What matters is that you take action, and you keep the promise that you made to yourself. "I am going to keep the momentum going and hit these goals."

Think about this. If you are earning $12,000 a month gross, 1% of that is $120. That's the cost of a nice dinner for two people. What if I were to ask you if you could cut out one nice dinner a month? Of course, you can still go out and eat, and do the little activities that you enjoy, but you can also bid that dinner a fond farewell! You and I both know that you can.

Sure, I know you can go without this dinner, but before you answer, if you can, have you thought about the other bonus to this plan? If you skip one meal per month, dining out, that's going to save you tons of extra calories in addition to saving you money.

We've all been there; we have eaten ALL OF THE THINGS while we are out for dinner, and then about fifteen minutes later, you're feeling like a disgusting pig. I know how you feel. This isn't a judgment. It happens to me all the time. It would be nice not to feel like that as much. At least, that's how I feel. Well, using this dinner as a metaphor, shouldn't you get the same gross feeling from overspending? When I cave in and have that big dinner, not only do I feel so full, I could pop, but I have to stare at that big bill the waiter or waitress brings over and stomach that!

Overeating and overspending are going to happen, but you have to stay the course (pun intended). You can't scrap your healthy eating plan because of one night's indulgences, just like you can't throw out your long term financial plan because of one instance of overspending. You are in charge of YOUR choices, nobody else. Ask yourself, *What do I want more?* Do I need to eat at a nice steakhouse three times a week, every week? That's a lot of money and a lot of calories. If you cut out two of those dinners, that would be a significant change, wouldn't it? And as we are learning in this book, there is no such thing as small change.

Consistency is key, and you can't keep making different rules to justify bad decisions. We all make bad decisions from time to time, and when we do, we need to resist trying to justify them to ourselves. Justifying bad choices leads to bad habits in any area of your life. Accept that you made a bad choice and don't dwell on it; just move on!

Simply changing a few small choices will have huge results over time. You will start to see the great results compounding, and this should motivate you more than ever. Each decision will lead you to be that much closer to becoming more financially free than you ever dreamed of.

If you want to get an understanding of how small changes now can pay out BIG TIME in the future, here is a link to my Investment Calculator. As a money nerd, this calculator is one of my favorite things in life, and I had it custom built for this book to share with you. I am sharing it with you because I want you to have what you need to meet the goals that you set for yourself from reading this book.

Please go to this site to access your Investment Calculator: www.paulhalme.com/investment-calculator

Make sure you use it. I promise that you'll be completely stoked to see all of the cool things that you can do when you move even a little bit of your money around.

You'll be able to keep track of your decisions, and of course, this calculator will help you to save. Better yet, when you see what you are capable of saving, you will *want* to save. Saving money has a weird side effect. When people start to see those numbers rise, they don't want to spend. The game of how much they can sock away gets even more fun, and they do everything in their power to stop spending and watch their savings grow.

At the beginning of each year, I review the previous year and how much my accounts grew. It's one of the biggest highs that you can feel, with the only side effect being extra cash in your accounts. I can't wait for you to experience this phenomenon yourself. Just get started now and make it a game, it's even more fun than watching your favorite team win because you know that soon you can access all that money you put away.

Chapter 6: Automation is the Key

"Do not save what is left after spending
but spend what is left after saving."
~*Warren Buffett*

Our subconscious doesn't want us to save money.

When we try and make a prudent and deliberate money decision, we run up against subconscious programming. Remember, money doesn't grow on trees… lol. It's these subconscious thoughts that hold us back from true financial freedom. I can still hear my parents in my head to this day. Our brains scream: *We have to pay all these bills first! Just leave the money here for the bills!*

And then your buddies call, "Let's go out!" Oops, that was a $150 night. "Oh well, money is evil anyway, and I'll never save anything, so why try?" The excuses just pile up, and we feel ok for a little bit. When that happens, we blow through all of our money ASAP, the situation worsens, and then we feel like we have to live by the "B" word. We already know budgets suck.

This is why you have to automate the savings function in your bank accounts so that every day you are moving a percentage of your checking account (or whatever account holds the money that you spend regularly) to your long term savings. Most banks allow this, and if they don't, find a bank that will let you do this. Most banks do a daily sweep and move money from checking to savings every business day. Once you contact your banks and have your daily savings sweep up and running, you are now off to the races. It becomes fun to wake up and see the money moving into your accounts; it's pretty much addictive.

Doing this means that you will know exactly what is happening to your hard-earned dollars. Watching your dollars grow makes it easier to stay on track. Having your savings automated will take care of any stress that you feel when you worry about money.

Automating your savings and accruing money will comfort you. There will always be stuff that can potentially happen to derail us in life. We know that there will always be fires to put out, but this plan will allow you to extinguish the fires and save money at the same time.

Think back to the many times that you have harbored worries in your life. I am willing to bet that 95% of what you have worried about never even happened. Knowing that, let's do everything we can to make a commitment to breaking the cycle of worry. We should also strive to try and break free from the scarcity mindset and being broke all the time. If you are going to break this cycle, then you must alter the way that you respond to change.

You can't worry about breaking your diet. You must stay on course with your overall commitment to eat better and try as hard as you can even when you fall off the wagon. When that happens, we know the best course of action to take is to get right back on that horse and pick up where you left off trying as hard as you can to stick to the plan. Take the same position with your money, and don't forget the key lesson in growing it.

You have to move money to make money. Therefore, you need to become comfortable with moving your money, or you can't grow it! Make the money moving step of your new plan, as simple as possible. For instance, move your percentage from business checking to business savings automatically using the daily sweep function from your bank, as we talked about.

Make sure that you don't need to actively think about this step so that you can get to the next step, one that I get even MORE super excited about. I can't wait until you keep your commitment to yourself with your money, and you are finally able to ask yourself at the end of the month, *Hey, where did all this money come from?* Wouldn't that be a much better question to ask yourself than *Hey, where did all my money go?* Of course, it would be.

Now, let's take a bird's eye view of that momentous occasion where instead of wondering where all your money went, you are wondering where in the world all the extra money came from. This is where we get our Money Math on! We will now reverse engineer your monthly savings amount. For example, if you are making $15K per month and your profit savings percentage is 10%, the monthly amount that needs to move is $1,500. The next step is to determine how much money needs to move into your savings every BUSINESS day per month. The average number of business days in one month is twenty-one, so $1,500 divided by twenty-one would be $71.50 (you can round up to $72 if you want). The number you wind up with is the amount that needs to be moved into your savings each business day!

It's so much easier to have $72 per business day move to your savings than to move $1,500 at the end of the month, don't you think? And if you think $1,500 is a large chunk to move in one swoop, imagine how hard it will be when you increase your percentage, and that number grows. See how fast this money can accumulate!

After one year of putting away $1,500 per month, you are at $18,000. Five years you are at $90,000. Ten years you are at $180,000. And now throw in a compound return of 8% annually, and in 10 years you are at $274,419.

Our subconscious is wired for us to be broke and scared about moving large sums of money, so by breaking those larger numbers down to smaller increments, our poor little monkey brains don't freak out!

Check out the graph on the next page to put it into an image for you.

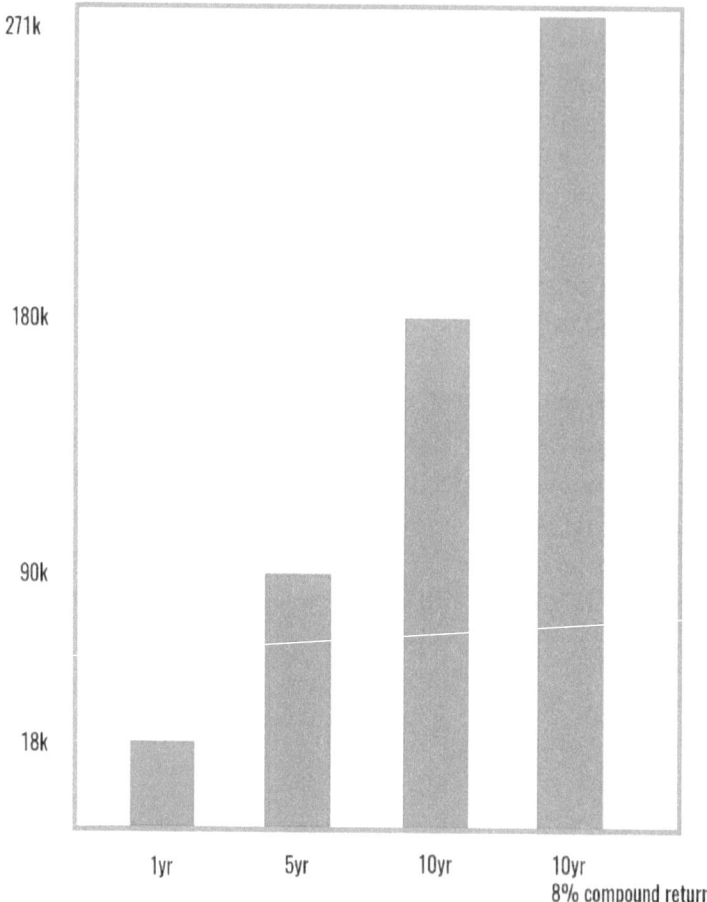

271k				
180k				
90k				
18k				
	1yr	5yr	10yr	10yr
				8% compound return

While I recommend that you set up this savings sweep to occur daily, that might not work for you. Depending on your needs, you might need to create a system that makes more sense. If you need to set up your sweep to occur weekly, biweekly, or even monthly, that's okay. Just make sure whatever your schedule for savings is that you set it up to be automatic.

Another bonus to the automatic savings sweep is that you have to make an effort to stop it from occurring. To stop an automatic savings transfer, you actually have to log into your bank account, find the settings, and manually stop the transfer from happening. While you are completing these steps, you have a lot of time to think about whether you really want to stop the sweep or not.

You need to have this step between yourself and the money that you are saving; you need a buffer. This buffer is critical in training your subconscious to stop looking for ways to gain access to the nest egg that you are creating. You know the old age question that asks, *"How do you eat an elephant?"* The answer is: *"One bite at a time."*

Your savings goal is a big elephant. You have to chip away at it consistently, or as it pertains to this analogy, eat it one bite at a time. Some people bug out if they have to transfer $1,000 in one go! So, you need to promise yourself that you will move the money in small increments, just like you will eat that damn elephant. Not feeling the elephant analogy. Maybe you'll like this one better.

In Amarillo, Texas, they have the 72oz steak challenge. I am a sucker for a good challenge, so I tried the 72oz steak challenge a few years ago. When they brought my challenge to the table, I realized that I messed up.

The meat of the 72oz steak apparently isn't enough to qualify you to win the challenge in Amarillo, Texas. You have to eat the sides that come with it, too.

To make it worse, when you engage in this challenge, you get to sit on an elevated table in front of everyone. As I sat there on this riser, I looked at all that food, and all I could think was *I can't do this*.

Since I had already committed, I knew that I had to give it my best, I attacked the steak, and for a little while thought I might actually finish it. Then with fifteen minutes left, the meat sweats kicked in. I was hurting. The meal was going so well, the steak was tasting great and then all of a sudden, I couldn't eat anymore.

It was like I was eating a different steak all of a sudden, it felt cold and undercooked. I was scared to try and choke it down and then have it come flying up in front of all these people.

At five minutes to go, I told myself, "*You can do this.*" There were only 6oz left, but by now, the meat was getting cold and so hard to chew. I was so close, but I didn't win the challenge.

I was so full, and now I had to pay $72 on top of it for not finishing. I was miserable and did not eat any food for two days. The thought of food made me sick, almost as sick as the thought of having to live my life on a budget.

The 72oz steak challenge is just like building your savings. If you told me to go eat a 72oz steak in one sitting, I would say no chance (because I tried that once and wanted to barf). I would rather eat six different 12oz steaks over the week; that sounds way better. Same as if I told you to put $72,000 in your savings in one shot. It's too daunting a task. You have to do it one steak at a time. You will be putting a little bit of money away each day. If you haven't done so yet, I want you to go online right now. Look at your accounts and see if you can set up the daily sweep. You should be doing a dollar or 1%, and as long as you have set up your money to move, that's all that matters. The amounts will change as you move forward.

Shoot for having a daily sweep setup from checking to savings, and before I talk anymore about this topic, I'd honestly rather have you take action and stop reading this amazing book. **Stop reading and go set this step up RIGHT NOW**. That is how important it is to me, for you to simply start. This step is so important to me, and my financial plan, that I have a daily sweep set up on my personal account as well as multiple business accounts. Every business account that I have (with a number of companies) is set up with a daily sweep so that my businesses are more profitable and able to scale.

What I am teaching you is the exact model that I follow, and I want you to do it too because it leads to doing more fun stuff. I still work hard, but then I also play hard. You can do the same thing and enjoy your life just as much.

For example, I'm taking a trip to Bali for a marketing conference. Years ago, there was no way I could have done that. Now, I just grab some money out of the excess business savings. Remember, once we have the six month buffer built up, you can use the surplus in that account for business expenses (please confirm with your accountant that it is an eligible business expense). I can feel good about it because I know that I have the systems in place to replenish that money automatically. I don't tell you this to brag. I tell you this because what I am teaching you is so simple that you can do it too.

I also tell you this because when you have such joys and freedom in your life, you want to share it with other people so that they can experience them as well. If misery loves company, well, so does happiness. In my case, I'm taking a business trip so that I can write it off. Through this savings method, I can go to cool places and take trips of a lifetime. I can see the world.

My best friend Travis Lutter, who runs a very successful school and has a good grip on money, hit me up the other day. He wanted to buy a new motorcycle (he already has five, I believe). Nothing makes him happier than riding. We talked about his finances, and I told him to do it. He does a really good job of managing his money, so I knew he could buy like ten of them, so it wasn't an issue.

But he was stuck. He said he couldn't spend the $26k even though he had it in his extra account. So, I told him that's cool, leave it in the bank and then when you die your wife's new man can spend it, he will thank you. He called me the next day as he left the bike dealership on his new ride.

I knew his financial situation, and this purchase wasn't going to affect him, but it was stuck in his head to keep saving. I believe you should save, but you need to live your life too. What I have shared with you, allows you to have a little fun, and you need that. We all do. Isn't that the point of life?

Setting up your accounts and plans is going to get you to the right place to be able to enjoy life, have more fun, and have so much less stress.

Let's get your mind even more right. After you read this, close your eyes and think about the amazing trip you want to take your spouse or kids on. What does it look like? How does the food taste? Are people different? What adventures are you going on?

Now, write down the date that you are going to take this trip! And it better not be when you are old as dirt. You need to live your life now!

Date of my dream trip: _____

Ready, set, go. Take action. I'll wait while you set up your daily sweep. Then we can start in on the next chapter. Building Your Future.

Chapter 7: Building for the Future

"Ambition is the first step to success.
The second is action!"
~Unknown

This chapter is very important now that you have the systems in place.

We have talked a lot about savings and determining the goals that you have for yourself. And in this chapter, I want you to think about building your future. Once you have the magic number of six months of expenses in your savings, account it's time to move to the next logical step: withdrawing and investing. We are now going to start moving money to set you up for long term success.

Here's how much to move: 50% of the surplus money that has accumulated on a quarterly basis will go into a long term investing account. The other 50% can stay in your business savings account.

REMEMBER: Do not dip into your emergency funds!

Your emergency fund is the account that protects you and your business. You only take money out of this account for a serious business emergency. The goal is to have at least six months of operating expenses in that account.

I don't subscribe to the "Don't buy coffee every day; you'll save $150 a month, and then you can retire in eighty-seven years." philosophy. I call BS on that plan, and here's why. I'd rather enjoy my coffee, save for my wife's and my retirement, and have a lot of fun along the way. I want to travel now and not when it's hard to get around or when I can't get around at all.

No matter how the rest of my plan turns out, I know that 50% of my surplus money is going into long term investing at a brokerage firm that's not at my bank. **I repeat: NOT at my bank.** There are a couple of reasons why we proceed this way, but the most important reason is that you want to make it harder to transfer that surplus money back into your business accounts.

This setup creates another barrier, making it more difficult to access your money. When you put money into your retirement accounts, then you absolutely don't want to take it out…unless it is a dire emergency. So, heed my advice, and keep your brokerage away from your bank. This is one of the biggest mistakes that I saw people make when I was a stockbroker. People would call up to take money out of their *XXX* accounts to get caught up on bills, or for things that an emergency account would cover. They didn't have an emergency fund, though, so they took money out of their retirement accounts and had to pay a 10% penalty to the government and pay taxes on top of that.

This would drive me nuts! For every dollar that they withdrew, they would only get sixty or seventy cents after the government was done with them. Hell, to the no! I am not going to pay more taxes on my money, and I always explain this ridiculous cycle to my clients. This is another HUGE reason why your emergency account is so important. Put the money with a reputable firm and let it grow!

Speaking of stashing your cash in a reputable place, you will need to look at a variety of different brokerage firms, and especially you should be on the lookout for low fees, low cost, and really good reviews.

Nowadays, you can get your account set up with no account fees, even no trading fees. Look to avoid any silly fees that eat up your savings and investments. Since there are so many different brokerages out there, it's hard for me to recommend one specifically. I can't in good conscience do that anyway (read the disclaimer). After you have selected your brokerage, keep following your plan. This will ensure that the process of funding your retirement account goes smoothly.

Not only that, but you will also start building an excess in your business savings account once you have your six months of emergency funds built up. You can use some of that money to fund new projects at your business, go on a trip, or take a course to improve your knowledge.

The overarching theme here is that you will now have multiple accounts where you are building your wealth and legacy. You can use the excess savings for whatever you want in your business, but please ensure that you are using the money to improve your business or life.

Don't take the money and go buy a Lambo so you can flex on IG to feel better about yourself...LOL.

Use the money to improve your business, take your family on a trip they will never forget, or fund a charity that really means a lot to you. You have to take care of yourself first. Like they say on the airplane, in case of an emergency, always put your own oxygen mask on first.

Now that you are clear on sweeping your account to create your savings, in the next chapter, we're going to break down how you can save for retirement and the different investment options and vehicles that you can use to grow your money.

At this point, you can start making plans for yourself, you can plan for your kids' future, and anything else that you want to do with your life. I have a special needs trust for my autistic daughter. Knowing that I can save this money and provide for her for the rest of her life and that no one can rip her off is something that helps me sleep at night. I believe that health savings accounts are a huge weapon to keep you from going broke, which is why I have one of those, too. When you're old, you don't know what limitations you might have, or what your day to day realities will be. My health savings account complements my health insurance.

You don't want to be unprepared.

Set up a health savings account (HSA) if you are eligible and fund the investment retirement account that makes the most sense to you like a traditional IRA or Roth IRA. These two things can change your life. They give you tax advantages and flexibility to take care of anything in life. Look for any advantage that you can get against the system for when an emergency pops up.

My HSA account has been amazing, and the fund grows tax-free for medical expenses (meaning all of your earnings are tax-free as long as you are using the money for qualified medical expenses). It's like getting a bunch of free stuff, and we all love free stuff.

My son breaking his arm was one of the worst experiences of my life. I was flying home from a marketing conference, and I got a text from my wife (this was back when I still used airplane Wi-Fi, now I love to disconnect). She was taking our son to the hospital; he was hurt really badly in a bicycle accident. Thirty-four thousand feet in the air, and I could do nothing but think the worst. When we landed, I rushed home to find him ok and in a cast. I was just so happy that he wasn't injured any worse.

Then all these medical bills started rolling in. WTF!? *How can this cost so much?* After multiple calls and negotiations, we got the price down to a little under $4,000. My wife was freaked out, *"Where do we get the money to pay for this?"* From our HSA account, that's where, because we had been funding it for years.

I felt so good at that moment. I wasn't complaining in front of my little kid, saying that we didn't have the money and asking him why he wasn't more careful (guess who did that shit to me). I just told him accidents happen, and I am glad that he was ok and that I had a plan for this. Talk about a stress reliever and a life lesson for my son about responsible planning.

I want you to speak to your tax advisor and a financial planner to figure out what's right for you because if you don't build up your money, your future will suck. I hate to be so blunt about it, but it's the truth. Sugarcoating the facts will only hurt you and make your life more difficult in the future, so you need to know what to do. You need to know that there are options available that will allow you to anticipate your needs and fulfill them.

Ask yourself (and I already know the answer to this because everyone would say the same thing) *Do I want to be an old person who barely scrapes by with nowhere to go and no way to take care of myself?*

When you are older, and let's say you get sick, worries about money can make you even sicker. It stresses you out and makes it harder for your body to heal from ailments. Give yourself the best shot at being the healthiest that you can be...and that means financially, too.

So, save. Then go out and have some fun. Keep that spark alive. Take trips. Have adventures. Take your spouse on their dream trip. Go see the world. Do all the little things that make life worth living. Here's your next job.

Before we move on to the next chapter, take a few minutes to set up an account at a brokerage firm or a bank where you do not have any checking or savings accounts. You will feel so good about putting that extra step between your money and you.

Your To-Dos:

Put money into a low expense investment account.

Check out IRAs, health savings accounts, college savings plans, and if you need to, special needs trusts, etc. Talk to a licensed advisor before setting these up.

In the next chapter, we are going to go over Investments and ways to make your life easier. Don't worry. I am going to make this as simple as possible for you.

Chapter 8: Investments

*"When you invest, you are buying a day
that you don't have to work."*
~Aya Laraya

By this point, if you've taken the steps that I have outlined for you so far, every quarter you are planning (or have started) to invest in your emergency account in addition to your savings.

This translates to you taking 50% of the amount over your six-month emergency baseline out of your business savings account and moving it to a personal investment account at a brokerage.

You are now so far ahead of your friends and peers. You have taken care of your family and yourself for the long term. Pat yourself on the back.

I know investing sounds scary, and your Aunt lost everything in the last stock market crash. We are wired to not succeed at this. People buy when the market is at all-time highs and then sell at the lows. When was the last time that you went to the grocery store and looked for the steaks that were not on sale, that were priced at a record high? Never, that's when. You have to think long term and don't chase what's hot at the moment.

Don't get caught up in the hype. Remember when Bitcoin was going straight up, and everyone was getting rich except you. *It's gone up so much, and I don't want to miss out.* So, you randomly throw some money at it because Cousin Larry says it is going to a million and then BAM! It crashes. Hopefully, someday it does yield a large return but stop chasing the highs.

Develop a long-term plan. Yes, I bought some Bitcoin and will sit on it and wait. I only invest, into speculative investments, an amount of money I would be willing to pile up in the middle of my living room floor and set on fire. It's way better on the nerves to know that you will still be fine, even if the investment bombs.

Investing long term should not be scary; just avoid getting caught up in the latest hype. Let's cover some basics that will make this easier for you to understand.

Asset Allocation: This is just a fancy phrase for your investment strategy. There are three general categories where you're going to put your money: cash, bonds, and stocks.

Bonds: In finance, a bond is an instrument of indebtedness of the bond issuer to the holders. The most common types of bonds include municipal bonds and corporate bonds.

Stocks: When you buy stock in a company, you're purchasing a tiny bit of ownership in the firm. Generally, the better the company performs, the more your share of stock is worth. If the company doesn't do so well, your stock may be worthless.

Mutual Fund: A mutual fund is a kind of investment that uses money from investors to invest in stocks, bonds, or other types of investment. A fund manager (or "portfolio manager") decides how to invest the money, and for this, he is paid a fee, which comes from the money in the fund.

Expense Ratio: The expense ratio of a stock or asset fund is the total percentage of fund assets used for administrative, management, advertising, and all other expenses. An expense ratio of 1% per annum means that each year 1% of the fund's total assets will be used to cover expenses.

Index Funds: An index fund is a mutual fund or exchange-traded fund designed to follow certain preset rules so that the fund can track a specified basket of underlying investments.

Dollar-Cost Averaging: This is an investment strategy that's implemented with the goal of reducing the impact of volatility on large purchases of financial assets such as equities.

Market Timing: This is the strategy of making buying or selling decisions of financial assets (often stocks) by attempting to predict future market price movements. The prediction may be based on an outlook of market or economic conditions resulting from technical or fundamental analysis.

Average Annual Total Return: This is defined as the average annual return that takes place over a defined number of years and assumes the reinvestment of dividends.

Compounding Results

"Compound interest is the eighth wonder of the world. He who understands it earns it; he who doesn't pays it."

~Albert Einstein

The power of compound interest is amazing.

You saw earlier in this book what compound interest could do, now let's break it down. If you put away $1,000 and with an 8% average annual return, that $1,000 will become $10,935 in thirty years without you doing anything. I know, thirty years sounds like a long time and can seem pretty boring until you start doing the money math on what's possible. Let's look at what happens if you put this money away monthly!

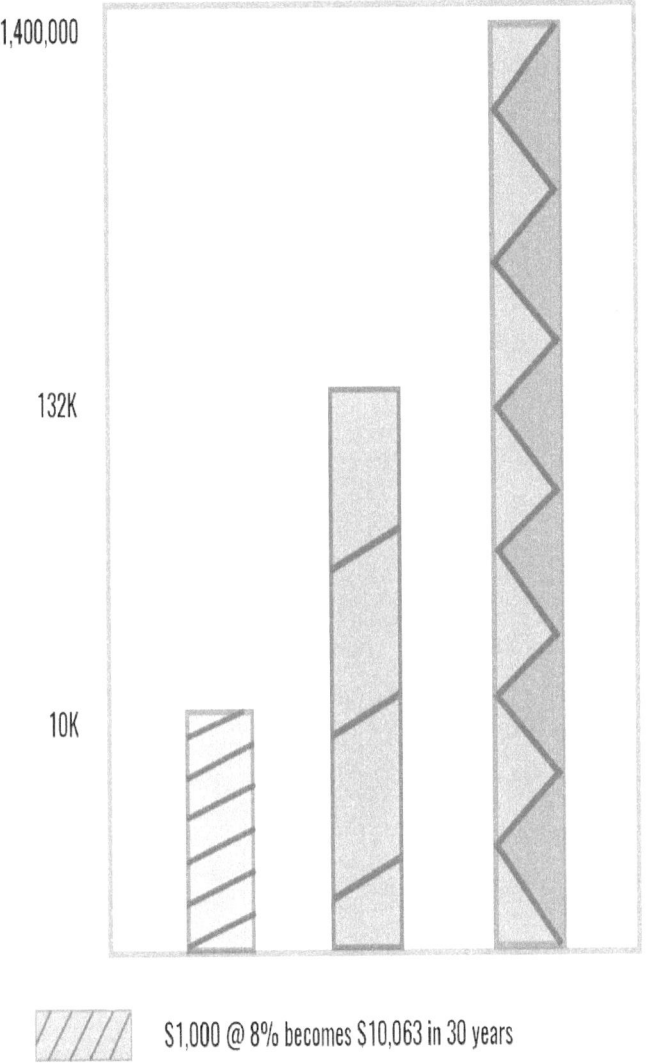

/////	$1,000 @ 8% becomes $10,063 in 30 years
///	$1,000 @ 8% with additional $1,000 yr $132,409 in 30 years
∧∧∧	$1,000 @ 8% with additional $1,000 per month 1,427,676 in 30 years

Money Math To Become A Millionaire:

If you put the $1,500 per month that we talked about from the last chapter into the S&P 500 each month, you would see some really amazing returns.

$1,500 x 12 months = $18,000. With an annual average return of 8%, that $18,000 now grows to about $18,674. I know, $674 growth is not sexy. But compounding is sexy as hell!

$1,500 x 60 months with average annual return of 8% = $110,215.

$1,500 x 120 months with average annual return of 8% = $274,419.

$1,500 x 264 months with average annual return of 8% = $1,075,182.

Twenty-two years to become a millionaire! The earlier you start, the easier it will be. If you think that compounding is sexy, starting to invest early and leveraging the power of time is even hotter!

Let's look at two examples to better illustrate how powerful time is: Boring Bob and Partying Pat. These two gentlemen are both twenty-five years old.

They both have good jobs and decide to become entrepreneurs. They both have businesses making $15k a month, and they are living a good life.

Bob starts following my system and is putting away $1,500 a month into his accounts while Pat is out partying and having a ball spending his $1,500 a month. Let's fast forward. Now, they are thirty-five years old. Bob has over $274,419 (with 8% average return) Pat has about $11 and a beer belly.

How different will Bob's life be if an emergency pops up or he just up and decides to take a vacation around the world? Due to a little planning and taking action, he has now accumulated some real money that will take care of him if either of these situations occurs. Would having 274K in your account help you make better decisions under pressure and relieve some stress?

Pat decides he needs to do something about his finances (or lack thereof), after seeing how much money Bob has. He mans-up and starts putting $1,500 a month into his savings account and begins to follow the system.

Soon, Pat is feeling great and can't believe how easy it is to build savings. It's all on autopilot, and the accounts just keep growing. Fast forward again. Now, Bob and Pat are forty-five, and out playing golf one day. Pat starts to brag about how he now has $274K in savings.

Bob is proud of him and tells him, *"Great job,"* with a little smirk. Pat wants to know what's up, and he wonders how much more money Bob could possibly have. It couldn't be that much more, right? *"A little over $880K,"* Bob replies when Pat asks how much more he has. Now, wouldn't it be nice to be Bob in this situation? I think so!

Bob is in a crazy awesome financial position at the age of forty-five. He could literally stop saving and investing (which I do not think he should do) and have over $4,300,000 in his account at the age of sixty-five with just an 8% average annual return compounded over the twenty years. He could take the money he is automatically investing and put that into his grandkid's college accounts, fund a family trust or donate to his favorite charity. The options are limitless since he has done such a great job with his plan.

Follow the plan and get the money!

This number would change most people's lives, and there is no reason you can't do this.

A beautiful occurrence in investing consistently is dollar cost averaging. Let me explain it this way: you're always buying into the market with dollar cost averaging, so if it's up or down, it doesn't really matter. The fact is, you're always buying in.

Instead of making one big investment and hoping you got in at the right time. Setting up a consistent investment plan makes it way easier to make money. Of course, it makes a bigger difference when you have a nice, fat account and a lot of money invested. As you're building, and until you get up into the hundreds of thousands of dollars, what you see when the market makes up, and what you see in the downswings are not going to make a big difference.

That's because you're always buying. When the market's high, you're buying it. When the market's low, you're buying it. This can take out the huge swings over time.

Do not try and time the market. The best investors of all time will tell you this repeatedly. Trying to time the market is one of the best ways to lose your money. Sure, there will be sell-offs, but you don't want to be the guy selling everything at the bottom. After a market corrects itself, the people who sold off at the downswing, miss all of the upswings as the market starts moving up again.

Then the market comes back, and it goes up above where they bought in before, but then they buy in because they have no choice over the matter. You always want to buy low and sell high, but the average person buys high and sells low. You can understand how this discrepancy would hurt you as an investor.

When you hang in with market fluctuations, dollar-cost averaging, long term planning, and investing with a plan, you are going to reap huge results and reduce a lot of stress as you avoid drastic swings, as well as the stress of selling and rebuying.

You should know before we go any further, and in case you get any funny ideas, that if you're trying to time the market, it's not going to work. Believe me, I used to be a trader, and it never works. Like I said earlier in this chapter, do not try and time the market! I hate to say this and don't take this the wrong way, but for the timing trick to work, you have to be a genius. You have to be Warren Buffet. He doesn't turn the market. Instead, he times his investments in companies.

Here are three popular investing strategies, two from a pair of very famous and successful investors and one that I became quite familiar with back in the day. (I can't recommend one strategy over another since we are all different and have different goals.)

Investor #1 is Warren Buffet, who says to invest in the S&P 500. It's hard to argue with one of the greatest investors of all time. Here's what he has to say:

Warren Buffett told CNBC on Monday that he's had a "Tough Time." trying to beat the S&P 500.

The Oracle of Omaha, who just released his annual Berkshire Hathaway (BRKB) shareholder letter, suggested that the index is still the best way to invest in the stock market for most people. He even joked that most of the time, he doesn't know how to pick individual stocks.

"I'd buy the S&P in a second," Buffett said, adding that he would give "enormous odds" that the S&P 500 will do better than thirty-year bonds over the next three decades.

Ray Dalio is Investor #2 and has an all-weather portfolio. He is one of the most successful hedge fund managers of all time. You can read a lot about his style in Tony Robbins' book Money. Ray Dalio's All-Weather Portfolio is supposed to be able to weather any economic season.

Find out how to build your own All Weather Portfolio and automate your investment so you can protect yourself against worst-case scenarios.

What is an All-Weather Portfolio?

The asset allocation of the portfolio is broken up like this:

- 40% of Long Term Bonds
- 30% of Stocks
- 15% Intermediate-Term Bonds
- 7.5% Gold
- 7.5% Commodities

Strategy #3, Target-Date Funds, have gotten very popular as of late. Pick a date that you want to retire, and the fund is managed to that goal date with asset allocation.

A target-date fund is a fund offered by an investment company that seeks to grow assets over a specified period. The structuring of these funds addresses an investor's capital needs at some future date; hence, the name "target-date." Most often, investors will use a target-date fund to apply to their onset of retirement. However, these mutual funds may find use in many portfolios that need to specify funds for a future event such as a child entering college.

Target date funds use a traditional portfolio management methodology to target asset allocation over the term of the fund to meet the investment return objective.

There are so many investment strategies out there, and I wanted to show you a few, but I cannot recommend one for you. This is a conversation for you and your financial planner because you need to make sure that you are investing your money in the best way for you.

Now that you've been armed with some basic knowledge, it's time to find a brokerage. This brokerage is where you will be investing the money that you move out of your normal day to day bank accounts. This is also where you will build the future for you and your family.

This money will be used for both retirement accounts and non-retirement accounts. Once you find a brokerage company that you like, it's time to sit down with them and create a plan. You can Google low-cost brokerages to start. And you'll see TD Ameritrade, Fidelity, Schwab, Vanguard, and many others. There are so many brokerages to choose from, and your decision should come down to personal preference. I don't recommend one over the other. If you stop by one of these brokerage offices or give them a call, you could say, *"I'm looking to do this, and that and the other thing."* Explain to them what you need, and they will help you because they want your business. Shop around, see what each brokerage has to offer you, and then narrow your choices down to the two that you like the most. Weigh your choice based on which one gives you the best service, which one has the best features, and which one has the lowest cost fees. Then set up your account with the winner.

That's your challenge for this chapter. Research a variety of different firms; narrow them down to two; visit each at a local branch; and finally, pick the winner and set up an account.

Give yourself one week to get this done.

I want this chapter to get you excited so that you can see the possibilities of what you can accumulate to live the life of your dreams while having fun. There is no better feeling than logging into your online brokerage account and seeing growth in your kids' college funds, your health savings account, your IRA's, and your nonretirement accounts.

Please! Set these accounts up and start working to fill them. The peace of mind that you will gain is priceless. Don't just read this book and not take action. I want you to reach out to me in ten years and tell the story of how much your account has grown and how your family is taken care of.

In the next chapter, we are going to recap everything for you.

Chapter 9: Recap

"You now have the tools to build financial freedom for you and the next generations of your family; now, you just have to take action."

~Paul Halme

Now let's make sure you get everything going.

Do not wait and say I will start tomorrow. None of this book matters if you don't take the action steps. If you follow my plan, it will change your life and the life of your family.

Set up the accounts.

Checking

Savings

Brokerage

Retirement

HSA (if you qualify)

Move the money automatically. Get this setup. You can divide the monthly total by twenty-one days, and you will be off to a great start building your financial freedom.

Set up your Quarterly transfer plan: How much money is going to leave your savings account each month? Where is that money going to get invested?

Build a massive retirement account. Find the investment strategy that is right for you and keep adding to your investments on a consistent schedule. Talk with your financial advisor at least once a year to make asset allocation changes or to update your new financial plan.

Enjoy the little things that make you happy.

Take some time to write down the things that you are grateful for. No matter what, there will always be someone doing better than you, but there will also be millions doing worse. When you have a bad day, take a little time and think about all of the amazing things that you have in your life. Then go and do something that makes you happy!

Take care of your future medical expenses. Set up an HSA if you qualify. If you don't, then set up another brokerage account and start putting money away and only use it for medical expenses. This will really cut down on the stress of getting unexpected medical bills.

Hopefully, you enjoyed this book and will go out and implement it. Please make sure to use the bonus materials to get even better results.

I want you to be able to enjoy life now and accumulate the funds that you will need later on in life. After my little sister died at thirty four years old, I learned the hard way that tomorrow is not guaranteed.

I want to leave you with three words to guide you. Bad things will happen, you will face tough times, but no matter what happens in life: **KEEP MOVING FORWARD.**

Paul

P.S. Take the TRIP too! Make sure to read the bonus chapter at the end of this book.

Acknowledgments

There is no way this book would have happened without so many amazing people in my life.

First would be my amazing family: My wife, Lori, who is the opposite of me and pushes me to be a better version of myself daily. My Mom, Anne, who I owe everything to; she built the man I am today. My little sister, Jane, who taught me what living is really all about. I miss her every day.

Finally, my amazing kids, Chase and Paige; every decision I make in my life is about them having a better future.

After my family, there are some amazing people in my life who pushed me to share my message. Travis Lutter, my best friend, who supports me in all of my crazy ideas and pushes me. Mitch Miller, who told me I had to write this book and share my systems. He pulled out stories from me that I did not want to share but, in the end, made this book what it is.

My two business partners Alan Belcher and Amy Magers, who I am lucky to work with every day. We get to impact so many people, and working with you two has changed my life.

Finally, this book would never have been completed or been so good without my editor Hilary Jastram. She developed the perfect outline to work with and kept me on schedule. When I would get burned out, she would push me to keep going.

Also, a big shout out to my friend Sarah Lachowsky who read this book so many times to make sure it didn't read like some boring personal finance book and made sure it was ready to share with my readers. You are an amazing person.

To all of these people, I am so grateful.

About the Author

"I can take just about anyone who will listen
and guide them to financial freedom."

To entrepreneurs, Paul Halme is the secret business weapon they don't want their competitors knowing about.

This Texas-bred, college golfer turned World Champion fighter admits to having a tough childhood, and that business wasn't always so easy. Like a lot of kids, Paul had low self-esteem, an unstable father figure, and even lost his sister in his thirties. Paul's success story started with a lot of pain.

From that pain, Paul used his business acumen to build his martial arts school into one of the most successful gyms in the US. This wasn't enough for the former stockbroker, and he began creating high six-figure offline businesses for his clients resulting in his consulting company growing well into the seven figures. And he did it all while helping his clients and living a lifestyle of his own design.

Most people would ride off into the sunset at this point, knowing that they crushed their goals in multiple areas, but not Paul. His true passion lies in helping people with their money. Paul works with highly committed people who have worked hard to build their businesses, but who need extra guidance and strategy to take it to the next level.

What he sees time in and time out is a weak money mindset, which is where he generates the most success for his clients. The most common results his clients attest to are more time for family, more money, and more time to travel while having a successful plan to financial freedom.

To date, Paul has become a bestselling book author, an international speaker, and a sought after mentor for business owners worldwide. His new book: *The Money Fight,* is a multi-industry favorite, full of practical wisdom and deep insights on personal finance, business mindset, and long term financial planning for everybody.

The Money Fight is winnable, no matter your situation. All you need to do is read the pages, wait for the bell, and then knock your money problems out COLD.

Bonus Chapter: How to Fly for Free

These are my travel hacking tips to get you at least three free flights per year.

Depending on your tastes, you could rack up anywhere between $1,200 and $1,800 a year in free travel. It can be even more if you travel internationally. I use this system every year, and it works like clockwork, giving me way more than three free flights a year.

For my twentieth anniversary, my amazing wife and I are flying to Bangkok, Thailand, in Business Class for under $500 roundtrip. These business class tickets would have run me over $23,000 if I had bought them like normal. That is something that I cannot stomach, so I continually build up massive amounts of miles in my account so that I can have experiences like this. There is nothing like being able to lie down in your bed with your pajamas (yes, in business class, they give you pajamas) 38,000 feet in the air after dinner and some good wine. The only problem with this is that you can't go back. Go on YouTube and search for Seinfeld episode 52, and you will see what I mean. My system is nothing incredibly fancy, but follow it, and you will get to fly for free at a minimum of three times per year.

Cashing in on these flights allows you to go to that conference or take your wife on that trip you both were dreaming of. You can even go to another tournament (in whatever sport you want) this year! The sky's the limit! (Pun intended.) You get so much flexibility when you follow this system.

Step 1: Choose a primary airline that could be any one of the major airlines that has routes around you. Most of the time, you're going to have a main hub to help guide you. I live in Dallas, (airport code DFW), so that's an American Airlines hotspot. If you live in Atlanta, it's Delta, etc. If you're in a smaller city, you will pick the one you use the most, and that has a good network with partner airlines. It just depends on where you are located and which airline you fly the most. The goal is to pick one airline and do your best to stay with that airline. I know it can suck sometimes and that airlines mess up all the time, but if you stick to one primary carrier, it's going to give you a lot of benefits that we're going to go over next.

Step 2: After you pick your primary airline, sign up for their frequent flyer program. Always use your frequent flyer number to book travel and start accumulating points and other rewards.

Step 3: Get a business credit card that accumulates points using the frequent flyer program and account that you set up in Step 2. Most airlines have a co-branded credit card; it might just take some digging.

I know some people say: *Oh, I don't use credit cards. Credit cards are bad.* Don't listen to them, I use credit cards all the time, and I get lots of free stuff. The only trick is that you have to pay your credit card off every month. Don't let your balances accumulate, and make sure to pay your credit card off every month. Do this, and you will score all kinds of free stuff.

So, now you have a business credit card, and you can start charging your business expenses to it. If you're charging $5,000 per month in expenses, that's 60,000 points a year easily two flights right there. You could earn more than two flights depending on your activity and the different benefits from the airline that you use.

Let's recap. Now, you have a business credit card that's linked to your frequent flyer card number, and you are accumulating points. See how easy this is? So, what's next?

The final step is to get a personal credit card that also has your frequent flyer account attached to it. In addition to accruing travel points, legally, you have to separate your personal and business expenses.

By linking both cards to your single frequent flyer account, you will collect points even faster! For example, let's say you're spending $5,000 a month in business expenses and $3,000 a month in personal expenses, that's $8,000 that you are fully paying off every month. You're not acquiring any debt.

You must always pay off what you spend and treat that credit card like a debit card. Do the above math with me; that's 96,000 miles and almost four tickets! This sounds like a lot, but these are very small numbers. Imagine if you're doing 10K and 5K, respectively, that's 180,000 miles a year!

Can you now see the benefit of this strategy? The points compound so rapidly, and you get so many free things. The only catch is that you have to be responsible.

You have to pay the cards off. What you'll notice is with a lot of these cards, is that they come with a lot of other benefits, too. You'll get a free checked bag, and many the cards nowadays give you free TSA Precheck, which, if you travel, is the greatest thing on earth. TSA Precheck allows you to blow through security so fast it's absolutely amazing.

By strategically using these credit cards in combination with your points account, you'll start getting all sorts of benefits. You can get rental car discounts, and other discounts, so many that I can't even name everything. You get the point.

PRO TIP: When you are searching for the best credit card for your free travel system, don't be afraid of the cards with the slightly higher fees, either. Why? Because some of the cards with the higher fees have even more benefits. For example, the credit card that I use for my American Airlines' frequent flyer account gets me free access to the admiral's club at the airport. This is a travel game changer. I can relax in the club, charge my phone, grab a snack, and even have an adult beverage before my flight. It makes travel so much less stressful. As you can see, the perks can offset the cost of some of these cards. Just make sure to do your research. To be honest, even the free checked bags make higher fees worth it. Focus on the perks you can pick up, keep using the cards to compound your points, and earn as much free travel as you can.

When you do this, and you get some free flights, I want you to message me and let me know. My email is Paul@paulhalme.com.

Yes, I actually check my email, and I'd love to hear your story about how you got some free flights because of what you read here and, of course, what you thought of this book. Don't be afraid to share with me how using my plan helped to change your life and made you start saying: *"Hey, where'd all this money come from?"*

That's the best ending of all.

So, go get all your frequent flyer accounts set up and start building up those points.

Think about all of the exciting places you will be able to go now. It's like getting a travel bonus each year from the Airlines. But most importantly, have some fun. You only get one ride in this life, so build your own dream! Don't buy into building someone else's dream; designing your own is so much better. Email me at <u>paul@paulhalme.com</u> when you get all of this setup. I am here to hold you accountable.

Disclaimer

Paul Halme is not a registered investment, legal or tax advisor, or broker/dealer. All investment/financial opinions expressed by Paul Halme are from the personal research and experience of the author and are intended as educational material, although best efforts are made to ensure that all information is accurate and up to date, occasionally unintended errors and misprints may occur.

Paul Halme expressly recommends that you seek advice from a professional. Please consult a Registered/Qualified Financial Adviser before investing money.

The information contained in this book is not intended to be a substitute for financial advice that can be provided by your financial advisor. Although care has been taken in preparing the information provided to you, Paul Halme cannot be held responsible for any errors or omissions, and we accept no liability whatsoever for any loss or damage howsoever arising.

References

1. Buffet, Warren. "Do Not Save What Is Left after Spending but Spend What Is Left after Saving.'." Millers on Fire, March 19, 2017. https://millersonfire.com/decrease-increase/.

2. Cardone, Grant. "WISDOM QUOTES560 POWERFUL MONEY QUOTES THAT WILL MAKE YOU WEALTHIER." 560 Powerful Money Quotes, n.d. https://wisdomquotes.com/money-quotes/.

3. Carlin, George. "The American Dream." The Art of Asking, May 29, 2013. http://www.cherylharnest.com/author/admin/.

4. LaMonica, Paul R. "Warren Buffett Says He Can't Beat the S&P 500." CNN Business, n.d. https://www.cnn.com/2019/02/25/INVESTING/WARREN-BUFFETT-SP-500-STOCKS/INDEX.HTML.

5. Tran, Tony. "Ray Dalio's All-Weather Portfolio (Quick-Start Guide, 2020)." I will teach you to be rich, n.d. https://www.iwillteachyoutoberich.com/blog/all-weather-portfolio/.

6. Washington, Denzel. "Money Doesn't Buy Happiness. Some People Say It's a Heck of a down Payment, Though." AZ Quotes, n.d. https://www.azquotes.com/quote/815299.

7. Williams, Geoff. "10 Financial Terms Every Investor Should Know." US News, n.d. https://money.usnews.com/money/personal-finance/articles/2014/09/05/10-financial-terms-every-investor-should-know.

8. "'When You Invest, You Are Buying a Day That You Don't Have to Work.' –Aya Laraya." Portfolio Management, n.d. https://www.cultivatewealth.com/services/portfolio-management/.

www.ingramcontent.com/pod-product-compliance
Lightning Source LLC
Chambersburg PA
CBHW020546220526
45463CB00006B/2210